Genistein

Potent Soy Isoflavone

Rita Elkins, M.H.

WOODLAND PUBLISHING
Pleasant Grove, Utah

1998

Woodland Publishing

P.O. Box 160

Pleasant Grove, UT

84062

Table of Contents

Introduction

In the midst of frightening figures which soberly disclose the alarming rate of breast cancer in this country (not to mention the epidemic of PMS, menopausal miseries and the threat of osteoporosis), the profound value of the soybean as a remarkable phytoestrogen remains relatively unknown.

In my view, every woman should be made aware that soy foods, which contain marvelous compounds known as isoflavones, could provide significant breast cancer protection, not to mention a list of other benefits related to female complaints. In light of the many health benefits soybean phytosterols offer, it is imperative this data should be shared.

After completing the research for this booklet, I was stunned at the number of medical studies that document the positive effects on women of consuming soy foods or isoflavone supplements. Had I realized the staggering influence that isoflavones exert on both the female and male reproductive system, I would have given my children soy milk rather than cow's milk throughout their childhood.

I remain rather perplexed—especially when considering the hundreds of studies regarding isoflavones from soy—and wonder why every American medical doctor is not encouraging their patients to raise their isoflavone intake. The facts overwhelmingly favor imme diately increasing our inexcusably low consumption of soy and isoflavones.

Isoflavones have so many incredible therapeutic benefits for women, and it is rather disturbing that medical science has not worked harder to get the word out. The enormous disease-preventing capabilities of soy isoflavones rank with some of our most powerful medicines and yet, their properties are rarely acknowledged by physi- cians. Moreover, a vast variety of phytonutrients found in fruits, veg- etables and herbs are only now beginning to emerge as scientifically credible phytopharmaceuticals.

After reviewing the multitude of studies conducted on soy com- pounds, it is safe to say that American consumers should be aggres- sively incorporating soy foods into their diets and taking isoflavone supplements on a daily basis.

Did you know that consuming soy isoflavones may actually make it possible to forgo hormone replacement therapy and the accompa- nying side effects? Are you aware that isoflavones neutralize the very dangerous effects of estrogen on breast tissue? These are just two aspects of soybean phytonutrients this booklet will discuss.

The Soybean: One of Nature's Most Extraordinary Foods

The relatively benign-looking soybean contains very high amounts of several phytonutrients and also serves as an excellent source of plant-based protein. Soybean consumption in the form of tofu, soy milk, miso, soybean oil, soy flour, etc. can clearly help to protect against certain cancers and cardiovascular disease (a property that animal proteins certainly cannot offer). Moreover, the extraordinary compounds found in soy work as impressive antioxidants, inhibit the action of certain damaging compounds, help to normalize cell replica- tion, keep hormones like estrogen from binding to breast tissue, lower cholesterol, and have significant anti-tumor activity (Axelson, Barnes, Brook). Including soy in a diet that also emphasizes whole grains and fresh fruits and vegetables is vital to not only maintaining good health, but warding off a number of potentially fatal diseases as well.

Unfortunately, typical American eating habits fall dangerously short of ideal dietary goals with isoflavone consumption ranking near the bottom of the list. While the superiority of eating soy foods in their whole state cannot be disputed, isoflavone supplements are certainly better than nothing at all. Realistically speaking, many of us will fail to eat soy foods regularly no matter how good our intentions may be. For this reason, using soy protein powders and isoflavone supplements may prove to be more practical. Whenever it is possible, eat soy foods in their entirety; if you fail, however, to incorporate tofu or other soy products into your daily dietary routine, consider supplementation. The important thing is to get the isoflavone compounds into the body, one way or another.

Interestingly, the isoflavones found in soy are not the only therapeutic compounds the bean contains. The phenolic acid content of soybeans combined with its saponins and protease inhibitors work to protect DNA, lowering the risk of diseases like cancer (Brook, Calvert, Dipietro). These impressive compounds may also stop the growth of cancerous cells in at least two other ways which may or may not be estrogen-related. It can be safely assumed that soy may help prevent cancer in both pre- and postmenopausal women regardless of estrogen levels (Barnes-1, Henderson, Koo).

Soy-Consuming Cultures and Disease

Diet is considered to play a major contributing role in at least one-third of all cancer deaths in the United States. The American Cancer Society and the National Cancer Institute have published dietary guidelines encouraging Americans to cut their intake of fat, and dramatically increase their intake of fiber, fruits and vegetables. Recently, a great deal of research interest has surfaced concerning how soy foods can reduce cancer risk.

In Asian countries such as China, Japan and Korea, the incidence of breast and prostate cancer is up to 10 times lower than here in

America. Scientists have concluded that this profound difference is due to the fact that the Oriental diet is full of foods with cancer-preventing properties (Aldecrutz, 2–3, Haenszel, Hu, Lee). It has been estimated that one in nine American women will get breast cancer. Prostate cancer rates in America can be up to 30 times higher than some Asian cultures (Peterson, Severson). One in 11 American men will get prostate cancer. Unquestionably, populations that commonly consume soy foods have dramatically lower cancer rates. The Japanese breast cancer mortality rate, for example, is only one-fourth that of the United States. Studies tell us that eating soy foods is directly linked with a 50 percent decreased risk of breast cancer in premenopausal women (Lee). Scores of studies which involved Asian participants concluded that eating even just a single serving of soy per day can reduce the risk of breast, colon, rectal, lung, stomach and prostate cancer (Messina-3).

The soybean is one of the most impressive members of Asian food staples. Interestingly, cultures who consume less meat protein and more soy protein are considered healthier when it comes to certain prevalent Western diseases such as various cancers, heart disease, diabetes, menopausal symptoms and osteoporosis. Genistein emerges as one of soy's most therapeutic phytochemicals and according to existing data, could lower the risk of prostate cancer in men and estrogen-dependent cancers in women (Akiyama-1, Bowen). The isoflavone effect on estrogen is nothing less than remarkable and helps to explain why the Japanese language does not include terms typically associated with menopause such as "hot flashes." The striking health differences between our country and Asian populations is attributed to soy consumption.

For thousands of years, the Asian diet has been rich in foods made from the soybean. Consequently, the typical Asian woman receives 30 to 50 mg of isoflavones per day. It is thought that just one daily serving of soy (i.e., one cup of tofu) may afford women significant protection from hormonally-induced cancers, a fact which dramatically illustrates the potency of soy isoflavones (Caragay, Messina-2, Wong).

Unfortunately, American women are lucky to get 1 or 2 mg of isoflavones which are inadvertently consumed from soy protein concentrates added to processed foods for texture or emulsification. Very few American women deliberately seek out soy products to add to their diet. Ironically, the majority of soybeans grown in the United States are used for animal livestock feed and most of what remains is sent to Japan for human consumption. While soy foods are full of nutritious and protective compounds, it is the isoflavones which stand out as therapeutic.

What Are Isoflavones?

Soybean isoflavones are phytoestrogens which are nothing more than natural compounds which have the ability to mimic and manipulate estrogen in the human body. The profound significance of the isoflavones found in the soybean was discovered in the 1970s. Clinical data uncovered the fact that Asian women were consuming up to 100 times more isoflavones than American females (Adlercreutz-2). Isoflavones are chemically similar in structure to estrogen. The two primary isoflavones in soybeans are daidzein and genistein and their respective glucosides, genistein and daidzin. Soy foods typically contain more genistein than daidzein, although this ratio can vary depending on the type of soy food consumed. Traditional soy foods such as tofu, soy milk, tempeh and miso are all considered rich sources of isoflavones and can provide up to 30 or 40 mg of isoflavones per serving.

The isoflavones found in soy should be an integral part of everyone's diet. They can help to reduce cholesterol, prevent atherosclerosis, protect or slow prostate and breast cancer, prevent the kind of cell mutation that causes DNA damage, inhibit blood supply to already existing tumors, ease menopause and lower the risk of osteoporosis. Isoflavones act as weak estrogens which, ironically, protect us against the very dangerous health threats of the estrogen women produce.

Estrogen: The Good and the Bad

Many women can suffer from what has been called an "estrogen dominance," which can cause a number of miseries as well as increased risk for potentially fatal diseases. Enduring very heavy periods, sore and tender breasts, water retention, bloating and serious bouts with depression—which are all directly related to higher than normal amounts of estrogen in the body—are more common for premenopausal women in their forties than one would assume.

Most of us are also unaware that a woman can have regular periods and not be ovulating correctly. Impaired ovulation can create a deficiency of estrogen-neutralizing progesterone. Over time, the uterine lining will never suffciently shed, leading to endometriosis, uterine fibroid cysts, fibrocystic breasts, bloating, depression, heavy or irregular periods and possible malignancies.

Symptoms of an Estrogen Dominance

Aside from having your blood or saliva tested, it is relatively easy to assess whether or not you may be suffering from an estrogen dominance. Symptoms are:

- breast enlargement and tenderness
- water retention
- heavy menstrual flow or irregular periods
- carbohydrate cravings
- weight gain (fat on hips and thighs)
- fibrocystic breasts
- uterine fibroids
- loss of libido
- PMS
- mood swings/depression
- certain types of acne

Is All Estrogen Bad?

Certainly, all estrogen is not bad. In fact estrogen is absolutely crucial to normal female development and reproduction. Estrogen is the hormone that initiates female puberty, causing the development of the breasts, uterus, fallopian tubes, etc. It also contributes to female fat distribution. Prior to menopause, estrogen levels drop causing an eventual cessation of the menstrual period. When estrogen dominates, a number of negative symptoms can occur. It can:

- increase body fat stores especially on upper thighs
- promote water and sodium retention in the cells
- contribute to impaired blood sugar levels
- increase the risk of endometrial and breast cancer
- increase blood clotting which raises the risk of stroke
- contribute to mood swings
- thicken the bile increasing the risk of gallbladder disease
- cause headaches
- promote the loss of zinc
- interfere with thyroid function
- contribute to excess and irregular menstrual bleeding
- decrease libido
- reduce cellular oxygenation

Why Estrogen Can Be So Dangerous To a Woman's Health

The hormonal workings of a woman's reproductive system can predispose her to developing certain types of cancer (Cassidy, Feguson, Henderson, Martin). The longer specific estrogen-sensitive tissue is exposed to estrogen, the higher the risk of cancer. For example:

- Women who begin their periods early and stop later than the norm have a higher risk of developing breast cancer due to the fact that her tissues have had a longer history of estrogen encounter.

- Women are less at risk for developing breast cancer if they go into menopause early or if they have their ovaries removed surgically which induces an artificial menopause. It must be stressed here, however, that the hormone replacement therapy which usually follows this type of surgery comes with its own set of possible negative side effects.
- A woman who has had few or no pregnancies also has a higher risk of developing breast cancer.
- The older a woman is when she first becomes pregnant, the higher her risk of developing breast cancer.
- Women who deliver their first child after the age of 35 have a threefold higher risk of developing breast cancer than women who bear their first child before the age of 18.
- Women who never become pregnant and women who never menstruate are three or four times more likely to develop cancer, especially breast cancer.
- If a woman has an abortion in the first trimester of her first pregnancy, whether it was spontaneous or induced, she is 2.5 times more likely to develop breast cancer.
- Women with fibrocystic disease can be predisposed to breast cancer.
- Exercising reduces estrogen levels which can cause irregular periods, although breast cancer incidence was reduced.

NOTE: Soy consumption can increase an average menstrual cycle by 2.5 days, which means a lower concentration of estrogen exposure of breast tissue over time.

What these statistics imply is that when certain cells bind with estrogen for extended periods of time, cellular mutation becomes more likely. The isoflavones contained in soy can help to decrease this detrimental estrogenic activity by actually substituting for estrogen on receptor cells.

The Remarkable Estrogenic Activity of Isoflavones

Isoflavones have the distinct ability to compete for estrogen on receptor cells. In other words, the body mistakes them for estrogen and so they are invited to take their place on receptors, paradoxically acting as anti-estrogens. Much in the same way as they mimic cholesterol, isoflavones actually fool the body into thinking that estrogen has bound with the proper cells, thereby protecting these same cells from contact with real estrogen (i.e. breast tissue). You can see why the less time breast tissue is exposed to estrogen, the more protected it will be against the type of cellular mutations that cause the formation of a tumor. The soybean has to be one of the most prominent phytoestrogenic foods.

Clinical studies have found that test subjects with the highest concentrations of isoflavonoids in their urine, were protected against both breast and prostate cancer (Noteboom, Newsome, Adlercreutzx-2). Women who ate 3 ounces of soy products a day, including tofu, miso, fermented soy and boiled soybeans, received adequate amounts of isoflavones and were afforded the maximum amount of protection.

The isoflavones found in soy work together as a group of intrinsically linked biochemicals which are designed to not only protect the survival of the soybean plant itself, but to biologically benefit the consumer. The profound physiological significance of isoflavones cannot be overly stressed. Genistein is considered the star isoflavone.

NOTE: Pharmaceutical companies have already begun to jump on the isoflavone "bandwagon," having developed a synthetic variation of genistein called ipriflavone. The idea of isolating or synthesizing what nature has designed as a whole synergistic array of compounds in a particular food must be approached with caution.

Genistein: The Most Potent Isoflavone

Most of the research interest in the anticancer effects of soybean isoflavones has centered on genistein. While eating soy foods as Mother Nature designed them with all of their complementary nutrients is always preferable, taking genistein as a single supplement may also offer significant health benefits. Genistein is considered the natural analog to the drug tamoxifen, which is an anti-estrogenic compound used to treat breast cancer (Golder, Jordon, Bowen, Carter). Tamoxifen is the synthetic counterpart to genistein and works to block the ability of estrogen to stimulate the kinds of changes in breast tissue that result in the formation of tumors. It is currently in use in a 16,000 woman breast cancer chemoprevention study by the National Cancer Institute.

Genistein has also shown the ability to destroy certain cancer gene enzymes that can change a normal cell into a cancer cell, while simultaneously inhibiting blood vessel growth to larger tumors. Genistein can diminish the possibilities of cellular mutations which can result in malignant tumors, especially in tissue which is estrogen-sensitive. Genistein is the isoflavone which bumps estrogen away from estrogen receptor sites on cells and inhibits an enzyme called tyrosine kinase, which is involved in the formation of malignant tumors (Akiyama, 1-2, Asahi). Moreover, genistein functions as an antioxidant agent that also has antiangiogenetic properties (Fotsis, Graf, Pratt). In other words, it can inhibit angiogenesis (the creation of new blood vessels which nurture tumors). Without a network of vessels, most tumors will shrink. Moreover, this effect may even prevent tumors from ever establishing themselves in the first place.

Genistein and Cancer

Hundreds of scientific papers published on genistein (300 alone in 1994) describe laboratory tests which demonstrate its ability to inhibit breast, colon, prostate, lung, skin and leukemia cancer cells.

These studies conclusively show that genistein directly stops the formation and growth of skin cancers and precancerous cells in the colon from developing into malignant tumors. Moreover, it also possesses strong antioxidant properties and scavenges for free radicals that can contribute to the type of DNA damage that results in the formation of a tumor (Sit). In addition to these impressive credentials, genistein also inhibits tyrosine kinase (TPK), an enzyme which when found in certain concentrations in breast tissue is considered a predictor of breast cancer.

In 1987, Japanese scientists demonstrated a remarkable property of genistein: the compound has powerful anticarcinogenic influences that every woman should be aware of (Akiyama-2). In addition to this specific effect, genistein also inhibits the activity of other enzymes which control cellular replication (Messina-3). One of these is called DNA topoisomerase, which is the specific enzyme affected by chemotherapeutic medicines administered to fight cancer (Okura).

Apparently we all possess certain genes which either initiate tumor growth or restrain it. Certain components in cells called oncogenes can either be suppressed, which prevents cancer, or stimulated, which causes cancer. DNA plays a profound role in this process and if it becomes damaged, can send out the wrong cellular signals causing the uncontrolled replication of mutated cells. All of us have specific genes which have the ability to prevent this phenomenon; we also have other genes (oncogenes), which when activated, set tumor growth into motion. Genistein has the ability to occupy breast tissue and prevent the triggering of oncogene activity.

As mentioned earlier, Asian women who typically ingest up to 50 mg of isoflavones per day have a much lower incidence of breast cancer. In essence, their diet provides them with daily protection against the physiological processes which initiate breast tumors.

Genistein also has the very impressive ability to act as an antiangiogenesis agent which means that it inhibits the growth of new blood vessels required to nourish a tumor. Angiogenesis is particularly applicable in Kaposi's sarcoma, and is a vital part of the survival of any actively growing tumors (tumors cannot continue to grow unless a new network of blood vessels is provided). The anti-angiogenesis effect of genistein causes existing tumors to shrink or grow at a much slower rate (Fotsis).

One other unexpected benefit of genistein for people with cancer who are undergoing chemotherapy is that it boosts the effectiveness of these drugs and seems to target cancer cells which are actually drug-resistant (Peterson, Takeda).

Summary of Genistein's Effect on Cancer

• As a weak estrogenic agent, genistein acts as an anti-estrogen by competing with human estrogen for receptor sites in places like breast tissue.
• Genistein interferes with activity of enzymes that control cell growth, such as tyrosine protein kinase and DNA topoisomerase.
• Genistein can inhibit angiogenesis or the growth of new blood vessels which in turn keeps solid tumors from growing.
• Genistein may actually boost the effectiveness of chemotherapeutic drugs used to treat cancer.

The National Cancer Institute and Isoflavones

In 1990, a National Cancer Institute workshop singled out five chemical classifications of what were considered anticarcinogenic compounds in soybeans. These were designated as phytosterols, phytates, saponins, protease inhibitors and isoflavones (Messina-1). Soybeans are also rich in phenolic acids, which also have anticancer properties. While all of these compounds are thought to contribute to the value of soy as a cancer-fighting food, it is the isoflavones which have piqued the interest of cancer researchers. The two main isoflavones found in soybeans that have been the subject of study are genistein and daidzein.

On June 27, 1990 an NCI Symposium was held on the anticancer effects of soy, and the conclusion drawn was that soy foods play a substantial role in cancer prevention. The participants of this gathering identified five anticarcinogenic compounds found in soy. Consequently, the NCI allocated $3 million for additional research on soy foods and their ability to protect the body from cancer

Heart Disease and Cholesterol Reduction by Isoflavones

While genistein can certainly be viewed as a potent anticancer compound, it also has a very beneficial effect on the cardiovascular system. Genistein helps to prevent atherosclerosis by working as an anticlotting agent. Moreover, it also inhibits the activity of smooth muscle cell replication which helps to prevent plaque formation on artery walls. In addition, its antioxidant actions prevent the oxidation of LDL cholesterol (Sitori, Van Raaij, Brook). Statistics have shown that adding isoflavones to the diet can result in a drop in cholesterol levels by as much as 35 percent. One study in particular found that a group of children in Austria with high cholesterol levels who were put on a on 30 percent fat diet in combination with 20 percent soy protein experienced a 37 percent reduction in LDL, with little or no effect or their HDL levels (LDL is the bad cholesterol and HDL is the good variety).

Once again, this study suggests that our health may not be solely impacted by what we choose to eat, but what we leave out as well. Obviously, the potentially bad effects of dietary fat may be neutralized to some extent by the isoflavones found in soy foods. This same type of phenomenon can be seen in Eskimo cultures who eat diets rich in saturated fat and cholesterol but have low cardiovascular disease. The thought here is that the essential fatty acids (Omega-3) found in the fish routinely consumed by Eskimo populations keeps cholesterol levels in check and may also help to prevent cancer (Karmali).

Menopause: A Western Phenomenon Only?

Technically speaking, menopause refers to the permanent cessation of menstruation. It is a Greek term that combines the words monthly and cease. It's important to remember, however, that menopausal symptoms can occur for several years before and after a woman's final period. Menopause is actually a three part process that cumulatively ends the reproductive life of the human female. The first phase of menopause is sometimes called perimenopause and can start as early as age 35 as estrogen levels begin to decline. Erratic changes in the length of the menstrual cycle and the amount of flow are common during these years along with symptoms typical of PMS, such as breast tenderness, irritability, forgetfulness, mood swings, etc. In fact, some people have referred to menopause as nothing more than a bad case of PMS. For many women, this can be the worst phase. Frequently, women neglect to link their newfound symptoms to perimenopause causing them to feel out of control and confused. For this very reason, properly anticipating menopause with good diet, nutritional supplements and exercise is critical.

Because we are facing the menopausal season for the baby boom generation and due to the fact that the life expectancy for women today has been raised to 86, more women will be experiencing menopause at the same time than ever before. The average age for menopause is 51.5 years. Statistics tell us that one-sixth of the US population is comprised of postmenopausal women. It is estimated the number of women age 65 and over will double by the year 2000—and 75 percent of all American women will experience menopausal symptoms. Estrogen agents are commonly used to control the symptoms of menopause. These symptoms are associated with the hormonal changes that accompany menopause. A majority of menopausal women in this country experience hot flashes and approximately 25 percent feel unusually fatigued or depressed. Most menopausal symptoms are caused by reduced estrogen and progesterone levels. Symptoms of menopause can include:

- anxiety
- fatigue
- headaches

- loss of sexual desire
- moodiness
- night sweating

- heart palpitations
- hot flashes
- joint pain
- urinary tract disorders
- skin dryness
- insomnia
- vaginal dryness
- weight gain

Because estrogen receptors are found in brain, uterus and breast cells, a drop in estrogen may cause some of the symptoms previously listed and even include forgetfulness or the inability to concentrate. Low estrogen levels can also be responsible for reduced vaginal secretion resulting in dry tissue. Interestingly, Asian women who eat high soy diets do not have the same experience with menopause that Western women do (Adlercreutz-4). The naturally phytoestrogenic effect of isoflavones may help to compensate for falling estrogen levels in menopausal women, resulting in minimal or even absent menopausal symptoms. Most Western women who are post-menopausal typically look to synthetic estrogen drugs. These drugs are often prescribed for menopausal miseries, even though their use comes with an increased risk of endometrial cancer. Trying to raise progesterone levels with medication can help offset this effect, however, this therapy increases the risk of several other cancers. Hormone replacement therapy for women is controversial, to say the very least.

Can Genistein Substitute for Synthetic Hormone Replacement Therapy?

The isoflavones found in soy may actually substitute for the use of synthetic hormones. Because soy isoflavones mimic estrogen, genistein offers women a safe and alternative treatment for menopausal symptoms. At this writing, three clinical studies are in the works which are designed to evaluate the effect of soy on menopause. One such study is being conducted Dr. Greg Burke from the Bowman Gray School of Medicine at Wake Forest University. Two hundred-forty women over age 45 who are experiencing night sweats or hot flashes drink a soy beverage each day supplemented with 1 mg, 34 mg, or

50 mg of isoflavones. The study closely assesses the incidence of hot flashes, night sweats, and mood swings. Two other studies involve 60 women with hot flashes who will eat either two chocolate soy breakfast bars that contain 20 mg isoflavones each, totaling 40 mg per day, or two placebo bars without isoflavones. These women will be evaluated over the course of three months.

The initial findings are promising and suggest that isoflavone supplementation (genistein) should always be employed first, before resorting to hormonal drug therapy. The potential risks associated with hormone replacement therapy (HRT) for postmenopausal women are substantial. The message to postmenopausal women should be clear. All the available data strongly suggests that using soy foods or genistein supplements is safer and less expensive than hormonal replacement therapy. There is no question that the availability and ease with which isoflavone consumption can be augmented demands that women seriously look at it as an alternative to prescription hormones. The fact alone that it not only helps to control undesirable hormonally related symptoms and simultaneously reduces the risk of the very cancers which are killing thousands of women, makes it a must. Something as simple as consuming 40 to 50 mg of isoflavones daily may do the trick.

If you think you cannot obtain 40 to 50 mg of isoflavone compounds per day through dietary sources, think again. Scientists at the National Institute of Environmental Health Sciences conducted a study with postmenopausal women who were given a variety of soy-based foods for 60 days. The number of isoflavones consumed by each woman was estimated to be over 200 mg. This study tells us that it may be easy to consume the amount of isoflavones we need by using a variety of soy foods. If you find that this is not realistic, then obtain a genistein supplement and use it diligently.

Genistein May Protect Against Hidden Hormones

Obviously, there exist a number of hormones which are not produced in the body that pose significant health risks. We now know that if we take certain hormones into our bodies which come from external sources, we increase our risk for certain diseases like cancer (Marshall, Setchell). Birth control pills have been linked with an increased risk of developing breast cancer. Oral contraceptives are considered a risk factor for breast cancer, cardiovascular disease and liver and cervical cancers. Drugs which use both estrogen and progesterone have also been linked with increased breast, cervical, and uterine and ovarian cancer in women (Robboy). Potentially dangerous hormones include not only pharmaceutical varieties but environmental and food sources as well. The effect of diethylstilbestrol, or DES, is well documented and clearly increases the risk of vaginal and cervical cancers in women who were exposed to the drug as fetuses. Moreover, male babies born of mothers exposed to DES have reproductive and urinary tract abnormalities, including undescended testes, which can lead to cancer. In Italy, from 1977-1979, an epidemic of breast enlargement in children was seen and was blamed on DES ingestion from meat sources (Kalach).

Even here, we rarely address the potential problem of hormonally fattened beef, pork and poultry which we routinely consume (Setchell, Welsohons). Because we may not be aware of potentially dangerous hormonal exposure which can result in an increased rate of hormone-related cancers, we should be using soy isoflavones like genistein to protect hormonally sensitive tissue from carcinogenic changes.

Soy, Calcium and Osteoporosis

If you are increasing soy consumption, the question of soy phytates and how they relate to calcium should be addressed. If you are using genistein supplements, the issue is not relevant. If you eat soy foods, you should know that the phytates found in soybeans actually bind calcium. For this reason, it's a good idea to take calcium supplements or eat calcium-rich foods at a different time than soy foods. Phytic acids found in phytates are very valuable and help to protect against cancer and a variety of other diseases. It must also be stressed that even though phytates bind calcium, eating soy actually decreases the body's calcium quotient. In other words, while it is true that soy lowers calcium absorption in the stomach, it also lowers calcium loss which is typical in protein diets that come from animal sources. For this reason, soy is considered an anti-osteoporosis food. Many women are not aware that a diet high in animal protein can cause the loss of significant amounts of calcium (Heaney). Normal consumption of whole soybean foods should not interfere with nutrient absorption.

Consuming diets higher in plant protein and lower in animal protein has been associated with a decreased risk for developing osteoporosis (Neuberger). Soy contains a very low amount of amino acids that contain sulfur, which consequently leads to more calcium retention in the bones. Ironically, protein which comes from a calcium-rich source such as milk can result in a greater calcium loss than soy foods. The phytates found in soy also help to scavenge for free radicals in the colon, contributing to less colon toxicity, whereas animal proteins can predispose the colon to putrefaction and eventual colon cancer. Moreover, these compounds lower blood cholesterol and prevent the absorption of excess iron.

Genistein and Kaposi's Sarcoma

As we mentioned earlier, soy foods contain compounds such as genistein that have the ability to control the abnormal growth of new blood vessels which are required for the survival of a solid tumor. The term that refers to the growth of these blood vessels is called angiogenesis, and genistein is considered an anti-angiogenesis substance (Fotsis). Angiogenesis plays a vital role in Kaposi's sarcoma, and provides vascular nourishment for any solid tumor which must rely on a new network of blood vessels to grow. Scientists at universities in Heidelberg, Geneva and Helsinki, analyzed urine samples from test subjects who were eating a diet rich in soy foods and found that their genistein content was substantially elevated. Genistein has a very powerful anti-angiogenesis effect in laboratory tests (Fotsis). The genistein content of the urine of Japanese subjects who eat plenty of soy foods is generally 30 times more concentrated than that of Americans. While the study did not recommend using genistein for Kaposi's sarcoma (a common side effect of AIDS), it only makes sense that its ability to inhibit angiogenesis would be beneficial (Markiewicz). Taking genistein supplements in combination with a soy-rich diet is recommended.

Forms of Soy

Soy foods can be consumed in the form of tofu, miso, soy flour, soy nuts, soybeans, soy milk and isolated soy protein products which are varied and can be quite appealing. One-half cup of soy flour contains approximately 50 mg of isoflavones. Soy sauce and soy oil are not considered good sources of isoflavones. If you want to use a soy protein product, make sure that it is at least 65 percent soy protein. Soy protein products such as some meat substitutes may have their isoflavone content altered by processing techniques and are not generally considered a good source of isoflavones. However soy flour and textured soy protein are considered rich in isoflavones. Second generation soy foods such as hot dogs and certain soy ice creams can be relatively low in isoflavones.

Dietary Guidelines

To get the most therapeutic benefit from soy, you need 40 to 50 g of soy protein a day for ideal cancer and cardiovascular prevention. Tofu or soy milk has about 7 g of protein per serving. Try to eat three 4 ounce servings of tofu or 3 cups of soy milk daily and use products that have some fat content.

- 1 ounce of soy chips or nuts contains 42 mg of isoflavones
- 100 g of soy flour contains 50 isoflavones.
- 4 ounces of tofu contains 80 mg of isoflavones

- 8 ounces of soy milk contains 50 mg of isoflavones
- Most soy foods contain 1 to 2 mg of genistein per gram

Foods to incorporate into the diet include tofu, soy milk, soy chips, miso, soy flour, soy protein drinks, soy nuts and spreads. You can put soy powder into any or all baking recipes. Soy milk products are now considered quite appealing and can be used for shakes. Tofu can be whipped into dips, sauces, spreads, desserts, fillings, etc.

NOTE: Soy protein concentrate contains a more concentrated amount of isoflavones. Genistein is the primary isoflavone found in soy protein concentrate. The amount of genistein present in soy protein concentrate averages from .48 to 1.51 mg per gram. This form of soy can be used in liquids and provides a good source of genistein. Cancer patients can use this more concentrated form daily.

Thoughts on Genistein Supplementation

Because many of us will fail to eat soy foods on a consistent basis, isoflavone supplements in the form of tablets or powders may be a more realistic way of obtaining these valuable phytonutrients. Look for standardized products made from soy isoflavone extracts which do not contain fillers such as sugar, salt or starches and are wheat, gluten, yeast and dairy product free. In addition, avoid using supplements with preservatives or artificial colors or flavors. Most extracts will contain approximately 15 to 20 mg of genistein, daldzein and daidzin. Taking two of these tablets with meals is the standard recommended dose. People with cancer should take substantially higher dosages.

Bioavailability of Genistein and Safety

Isoflavones are orally absorbed, and genistein is excreted in the urine after circulating through the bloodstream. Soy isoflavones are considered safe and nontoxic if used as directed.

Complementary Agents

Natural progesterone creams (wild yam), indole-3-carbinol, vitamin E, evening primrose oil, saw palmetto, pygeum, black cohosh, alfalfa, red clover, licorice, fennel, anise, dong quai, fiber supplements.

Conclusion

In all the years of research I've done regarding natural medicinal compounds, soy isoflavones stand out as truly remarkable phytonutrients. As I alluded to earlier, I am angry that our physicians are not touting their benefits to both their male and female patients. Women in our culture live in fear of diseases like breast cancer, deal with horrific hormonally-related disorders such as PMS, are prone to heart disease, find menopause difficult, and believe that estrogen replacement therapy is their only option. Making sure that genistein consumption is adequate on a daily basis may well do more to help women manage these estrogen-related maladies than any other single dietary or pharmaceutical intervention.

The data from Asian populations is clear. Soybeans are an extraordinary food which women in western cultures need to acquaint themselves with. Taking a genistein supplement or learning to like soy foods is certainly a small thing to do taking into consideration the remarkable health benefits gleaned. I did not have to finish my research before I educated myself to soy foods available and the various genistein products on the market. As someone who is approaching menopause, I can assure you that I have become soy-conscious and that I am actively spreading the word.

References

Adlecreutz, H. Diet and breast cancer. Acta Oncologica, 31(2): 175-81, 1992.

Adlercreutz, H., et al. Lignan and phytoestrogen excretion in Japanese consuming traditional diet. Scand J Clin Invest 48:190, 1988.

Adlercreutz, H., et al. Excretion of the lignans enterolactone and enterodiol and of equol in omnivorous and vegetarian women and in women with breast cancer. Lancet 2:1295-1299, 1982.

Adlercreutz, H. Dietary phyto-estrogens and the menopause in Japan. Lancet 339:1233, 1992.

Akiyama, T., et al. Use and specificity of genistein as inhibitor of protein-kinases. Meth Enzymol 201:362-370, 1991.

Akiyama, T., et al. Genistein, a specific inhibitor of tyrosine-specific protein kinase. J Biol Chem 262:5592-5595, 1987.

Amaral MC, Miles S, Kumar G, and Nel AE. Oncostatin-M stimulates tyrosine protein phosphorylation in parallel with the activation of p42MAPK/ERK-2 in Kaposi's cells. Evidence that this pathway is important in Kaposi cell growth. Journal of Clinical Investigation, August 1993; volume 92(2):848-857.

Asahi, M. et al. Thrombin-induced human platelet aggregation is inhibited by protein tyrosine kinase inhibitors ST 638 and genistein. Feb. 309:10-14, 1992.

Axelson, M., et al. Soya—a dietary source of the nonsteroidal oestrogen equol in man and animals. J Endocrinol 102:49-56, 1984.

Barnes, S. Soybeans inhibit mammary tumors in models of breast cancer. Progress in Clin and Biological Research, 347:239-53, 1990.

Barnes, S., et al. Soybeans inhibit mammary tumor growth in models of breast cancer. In Mutagens and carcinogens in the diet. MW Pariza, ed 239-253, Wiley-Liss, NY, 1990.

Bibbo, et al. Higher risk of breast cancer in mothers given DES during pregnancy, 1978. A twenty-five year follow up study of women exposed to DES during pregnancy. NEJM 298:763-7.

Bickoff EM, et al. Relative potencies of several estrogen-like compounds found in forages. Agric Food Chem 10:410-412, 1962.

Biggers, JD, et al. Oestrogenic activity of subterranean clover. Biochem J. 58:278-282, 1954.

Block, G. Fruits, vegetables, and cancer prevention: a review of the epidemiological evidence. Nutrition and Cancer, 18:1-29, 1992.

Bowen, R., et al. Antipromotional effect of the soybean isoflavone genistein. Proc Am Assoc Cancer Res 34:555 (Abstr 3310), 1993.

Braden AWH, et al. The oestrogenic activity and metabolism of certain isoflavones in sheep. Aust J Agric Res 18:335-348, 1967.

Brook, JG, et al. Dietary soya lecithin decreases plasma triglyceride levels and inhibits collagen and ADP-induced platelet aggregation. Biochem Med Metab Biol 35:31-39, 1986.

Calloway, DH, et al. Reduction of intestinal gas-forming properties of legumes by traditional and experimental food processing methods. J Food Sci 36:251-255, 1971.

Calvert, GD, et al. A trial of the effects of soya-bean flour and soya-bean saponins on plasma lipids, fecal bile acids and neutral sterols in hypercholesterolemic men. Br J

Nutr 45:277-281, 1981.

Cancer Facts and Figures—1992. American Cancer Society. Atlanta, GA, 1992.

Caragay, A.B. Cancer preventive foods and ingredients. Food Technology 1992; 46:65-68.

Carroll, KK. Review of clinical studies on cholesterol lowering response to soy protein. JADA 91:820-827, 1991.

Carter, MW, et al. Estimation of estrogenic activity of genistein obtained from soybean meal. Proc Soc Exp Biol Med 84:506-507, 1953.

Cassidy, A., et al. Biological effects of plant estrogens in premenopausal women. Fed Am Soc Exp Biol 7 (abstr): A866, 1993.

Cheng, E., et al. Burroughs W. Estrogenic activity of isoflavone derivatives extracted and prepared from soybean oil meal. Science 118:164-165, 1953.

Cheng, E., et al. Burroughs W. Estrogenic activity of some isoflavone derivatives. Science 120:575-576, 1954.

Elias, R., et al. Antimutagenic activity of some saponins isolated from Calendula officianalis L, C, arvenis L, and Hedera helix L. Mutagenesis 5:327-331, 1990.

Farmakalidis, E., et al. Oestrogenic potency of genistein and daidzin in mice. Fd Chem Tox 23:741-745, 1985.

Fenwick, DE, et al. Saponin content of food plants and some prepared foods J. Sci Food Agric 34:186-191, 1983. Oakenful, D. Saponins in Food—a review. Food Chem 6:19-40, 1981.

Ferguson, DJP, et al. Morphological evaluation of cell turnover in relation to the menstrual cycle in the "resting" human breast. Br J Cancer 44:177-181, 1981.

Folman, Y., et al. The interaction in the immature mouse of ptentoestrogens with coumestrol, genistein and other utero-vaginotrophic compounds of low potency. J. Endocrinol 34:215-225, 1966.

Fotsis, T. et al. Genistein, a dietary derived inhibitor of in vitro angiogenesis. Proc Natl Acad Sci USA 90:2690-2694, 1993.

Frenkel, K., et al. Chymotrypsin-specific protease inhibitors decrease H2O2 formation by activated human polymorphonuclear leukocytes. Carcinogenesis 8:1207-1212, 1987

Gaddi, A., et al. Dietary treatment for familial hypercholesterolemia–differential effects of dietary soy protein according to the apolipoprotein E phenotypes. Am J Clin Nutr 53:1191-1196, 1991.

Golder, MP, et al. Plasma hormones in patients with advanced breast cancer treated with tamoxifen. Eur J cancer 12:719-723, 1976.

Graf E, Eaton, JW. Antitoxin functions of phytic acid. Free Rad Biol Med 8:61-69, 1990.

Haenszel, W., et al. Stomach cancer among Japanese in Hawaii. JNCI 49:969-988, 1972.

Harland, BF, Oberleas, D. Phytate in Foods Wld Rev Nutr Diet 32:235-259, 1987.

Hayakawa, K., et al. Effects of soybean oligosaccharides on human fecal flora. Micro Ecol in Health and Disease 3:293-303, 1990.

Heaney, R.P: Calcium in the prevention and treatment of osteoporosis J Int Med 1992.

Henderson, et al. Endogenous hormones as major factor in human cancer. Cancer Research 42:3232-3239, 1982.

Herbst, Haagenson, C.D. Disease of the Breast. New York: W.B. Saunders Co. Boyd, N.F., et al. 1988.

Hodges, RE, et al. Dietary carbohydrates and low cholesterol diets: effects on serum lipids of man. Am J Clin Nutr 20:198, 1967.

Howe, G.E. Dietary factors and risk of breast cancer. J NCI 82(7):561-69,1990.

Hu J, et al. Diet and cancer of the colon and rectum: a case-control study in China. Inter J Epidemiol 20:362-367, 1991.

Increased incidence of cervical and vaginal dysplasia in 3980 DES exposed young women. JAMA 252:2979-2990.

Ito, A., et al. Effects of soy products in reducing risk of spontaneous and neutron-induced liver tumors in mice. Int J. Oncol 2:773-776, 1993.

Ito, A. Is miso diet effective for radiation injuries? MisoSci and Tech 39:71-84, 1991.

Jackson, RL, et al. Antioxidants: a biological defense mechanism for the prevention of atherosclerosis. Medicinal Res Rev 13:161-182, 1993.

Kanazawa, T., et al. Anti-atherogenicity of soybean protein. Ann NY Acad Sci 676:202-214, 1993.

Johnson LT, Fenwick GR. UK mean daily intakes of saponins–intestine permeabiliziang factors in legumes. Food Sci Nutr 42F:111-116, 1988.

Jordon, VC, et al. Endocrine effects of adjuvant chemotherapy and long term tamoxifen administration of node-positive patients with breast cancer. Cancer Res 47:624-630, 1987.

Kalach, et al., Italian baby food containing DES:Three years later. Lancet (May 5): 1013-1014.

Karmali, R.A. Omega-3 fatty acids and cancer. J Int Med 225 (suppl. 1):197-200, 1989.

Kitts, DD, et al. Uterine weight changes and 3H-uridine uptake in rats treated with phytoestrogens. Can J Animal Sci 60:531-534, 1980.

Knuiman, JT, et al. Lecithin intake and serum cholesterol. Am J Clin Nutr 49:266-268, 1989.

Konda, K., et al. Induction of in vitro differentiation of mouse embryonoal carcinoma (F9) cells by inhibitors of topoisomerases. Cancer Res 51:5398-5404, 1991.

Koo, LC. Dietary habits and lung cancer risk among Chinese females in Hong Kong who never smoked. Nutr Cancer11:155-172, 1988.

Koury, SD, et al. Soybean proteins for human diets? J Am Diabet Assoc. 52:480-484, 1968.

Kunitz, M. Crystallization as a trypsin inhibitor from soybean. Science 101:668-669, 1945

Leaf, A. Cardiovascular effects of omega-3 fatty acids. NEJM 1988; 318:549-57.

Lee HP, et al. Dietary effects on breast cancer risk in Singapore. Lancet 337:1197-1200, 1991.

Liange, et al. Reduction in the risk of ovarian cancer associated with Oral Contraceptive use. NEJM 316:650-55, 1983.

Liener, IE. Factors affecting the nutritional quality of soya products. J Am Oil Chem Soc 58:406-415, 1981.

Loizzo, et al. Seminal and epidymal cysts in young men with known DES exposure in utero. JAMA 249: 1325-1326.1984.

Markiewicz L, Garey J, Adlercreutz H, Gurpide E. J Steroid Biochem Molec Biol 45:399, 1993.

Marshall, E. Search for a killer: focus shifts from fat to hormones. Science 259:818-821, 1993.

Martin, PM, et al. Phytoestrogen interaction with estrogen receptors in human breast cancer cells. J Endocrinol 103:1860-1867, 1978.

Mayr U., et al. Validation of two in vitro test systems for estrogenic activities with zearlenone, phytoestrogens and cereal extracts. Toxicology 74:135-149, 1992.

Meinertz, H., et al. Soy protein and casein in cholesterol enriched diets: effects on plasma lipoproteins in normolipidemic subjects. Am J Clin Nutr 50:786-793, 1989.

Meinertz, H. et al. Effects of soy protein and casein in low cholesterol diets on plasma lipoproteins in normolipidemic subjects. Atherosclerosis 72:63-70, 1988.

Messadi, DV, et al. Inhibition of oral carcinogenesis by a protease inhibitor. JNCI 76:447-452, 1986.

Messina, MJ, et al. Soybean intake and cancer risk: a review of the in vitro and in vivo data. Nutr Cancer. Manuscript.

Messina, The Simple Soybean and Your Health. Avery Publishing Group, 174, 1994.

Millington, AJ, et al. Bioassay of annual pasture legumes. The oestrogenic activity of nine strains of Trifolium subterranean L. Aust J. Agric Res 15:527, 1964.

Morley, FHW, et al. Proc NW Soc Anim Prod 28:11-17, 1968

Morrison, LM. Serum cholesterol reduction with lecithin. Geriatrics 13:12-19, 1958.

Nagai, M., et al. Relationship of diet to the incidence of esophageal and stomach cancer in Japan. Nutr Cancer 3:257-268, 1982.

Naim, M, et al. Soybean isoflavones, characterization determination and antifungal activity. J Ag Food Chem 22:806-810, 1974.

Nakashima H, et al. Inhibitory effect of glycosides like saponin from soybean on the infectivity of HIV in vitro. AIDS 3:655-658, 1989.

Natalie Angier. New York Times Science Times p. B5. April 13, 1993.

Neuberger, Wilcox, G., et al. Oestrogenic effects of plant foods in postmenopausal women. British Medical Journal 301, 1990.

Newmark HL, et al. Plant phenolics as inhibitors of mutational and percarcinogenci events. Can J Physiol Pharmacol 65:461-466, 1987.

Newmark, HL, et al. a hypothesis for dietary components as blocking agents of chemical carcinogeneis: plant phenolics and pyrolle pigments. Nutr Cancer 6:58-70, 1984.

Nielsen, F.H. Boron–an overlooked element of potential nutritional importance. Nutrition Today, January/February 1988: 4-7.

Noteboom, WE, et al. Estrogenic effect of genistein and coumestrol diacetate. J Endocrinol 73:736-743, 1963.

Oakenfull, D. Saponins in Food—a review. Food Chem 6:19-40, 1981.

Ogawara, H., et al. A specific inhibitor for tyrosine protein kinase from pseudomonas. J. Antibiot 39:606-608, 1986

Ohominami, H., et al. Effect of soya saponin on lipid metabolism. Proc Symp Wakan-Yaku 14:157-162, 1981.

Okura A, Arakawa H, Oka H, Yoshinai T, Monden Y. Biochem Biophys Res Comm 157:183, 1988.

Olson, A.C. Nutrient composition of and digestive response to whole and extracted dry beans. J Ag and Food Chem, 30:26-32, 1982.

Oral Contraceptives and hepatocellular carcinoma. Br Med Jour, 292:1355-1361. Cancer and steroid hormone study for CDC. 1987.

Oral Contraceptives and Breast Cancer Br J Hosp Med 30:278-83. Royal College of General Practitioners. 1981.

Osborene TB, Mendel LB. The use of soybean as a food. J. Biol. Chem 32:369-387, 1917.

Paterson AHG, et al. Can tamoxifen prevent breast cancer? Can Med Assoc J 148:141-144, 1993.

Perel, E, Lindner, HR. Dissociation of uterotrophic action from implanting inducing activity in two non-steroidal oestrogens (coumestrol and genistein). J Reprod Fert 21:171-175,

Petersen, Greg, et al. The Prostate, Volume 22, 1993, 335-345.

Peterson G, Barnes S. Biochem Biophys Res Comm 179:661, 1991.

Phillipy, BG, Johnston MR, Tao S-H, Fox MRS, Inositol Phosphates in Processed Foods J Food Sci 53:496-499, 1988.

Pixley, F., et al. Effect of vegetarianism on development of gall stones in women. Br Med J 291:11-12, 1985

Pool C. A case-control study of diet and colon cancer. Dissertation. Harvard School of Public Health. Boston, 1989.

Potter, SM, et al. Depression of plasma cholesterol in men by consumption of baked products containing soy protein. Am J Clin Nutr 1993.

Potter, JD, Topping DL, Oakenfull D. Soya, Saponins and Plasma Cholesterol. Lancet 223, January 27, 1979.

Pratt, DE, et al. Source of antioxidant activity of soybeans and soy products. J. Food Sci 44:1720-1722, 1979.

Proceedings from the Rutgers University Designer Foods III: Phytochemicals in Garlic, Soy and Licorice, Research Update and Implications May 23, 1994, WA DC.

Prospective study of Estrogen Replacement Therapy and Risk of Breast Cancer in Postmenopausal Women. JAMA 264(20):2648-53, 1990.

Rackis JJ. Flatulence caused by soya and its control through processing. JOACS 58:503-509, 1981.

Rackis JJ. Significance of soya trypsin inhibitors in nutrition. JAOCS 58:495-501, 1981.

Racks, JJ, et al. Soybean factors relating to gas production by intestinal bacteria. J Food Sci 35:634-639, 1970.

Ramakrihna MBV, et al. Determination of phenolic acids in different soybean varieties by reversed phase high performance liquid chromatography. J Fd Sci Technol 26:154-155, 1989.

S. Robboy, et al. Risk of breast, uterus, and ovarian cancer in women receiving medroxyprogesterone injections JAMA 249:2909-12, 1984.

Setchell, KDR, et al. Nonsteroidal estrogens of dietary origin: possible roles in hormone-dependent disease. Am J. Clin Nutr 40:569-578, 1984.

Severson, RK, et al. A prospective study of demographics, diet and prostate cancer among men of Japanese ancestry in Hawaii. Cancer Res 49:1857-1860, 1989.

Shutt, DA, et al. Steroid and phytoestrogen binding to sheep uterine receptors in vitro. Je Endocrinol 52:299-310, 1972.

Sirtori, CR, et al. Soybean-protein diet in the treatment of type-II hyperlipoproteinaemia. Lancet 5:275-277, 1977.

Sit K-H, et al. Effects of genistein on ATP induced DNA synthesis and intracellular alkalinization in Chang liver cells. Japan J Pharmacol 57:1109-1111, 1991.

Somjen, D, et al. Specificities in the synthesis of cytoplasmic estrogen-induced uterine protein. Mol Cell Endocrinol 4:353-358, 1976.

St Clair, WH, Billings, PC, Carew, JA, Obsested-McGandy, C., Newberne P., Kennedy, AR. Suppression of dimethylhydrazine-induced carcinogenesis in mice by dietary addition of the Bowman-Birk protease inhibitor. Cancer Research 50:580-586, 1990.

Steinmetz, K.A.: Vegetables, fruit and cancer. I. Epidemiology. Cancer Causes Control 1991; 2(50):325-57, and II: Mechanisms. 2(6):427-42.

Swanson CA, et al. Dietary determinants of lung-cancer risk: results from a case-control study in Yunnan province, China. Int J. Cancer 50:876-880, 1992.

Tackis, JJ, et al. Flavor and flatulence factors in soybean protein products. J Agr Food Chem 18:977-982, 1970.

Takeda Y., Nishio K, Nhtani H., Saijo N. Int J Cancer 57:229, 1994.

Tanizam, H., et al. Inhibitory effect of soya saponins on the increase of lipid peroxide by adriamycin (ADR) in mice. Proc Symp Wakan-Yaku 15:119-123, 1982.

Tokuda, H., et al. Inhibitory effects of 12-O-tetrdecanoylphorbol-13-acetate and teleocidin B induced Epstein-Barr virus by saponin and its related compounds. Cancer Lett 40:309-317, 1988.

Tompkins, RK., et al. Relationship of biliary phospholipid and cholesterol concentrations to the occurrence and dissolution of human gallstones. Annals Surg 172:936-945, 1970.

Troll, W., Wiesner, R., Shallabarger, CJ.Holtzmn, S., Stone, J.P. Soybean diet lowers breast tumor incidence in irradiated rats. Carcinogenesis 1:469-472, 1980.

Van Raaij, JMA, et al. Effects of casein versus soy protein diets on serum cholesterol and lipoproteins in young healthy volunteers. Am J Clin Nutr 34:1261-1265.

Vessey, et al. Neoplasia of the cervix uteri and contraception: a possible adverse effect of the pill. Lancet (Oct 22): 930-34, 1983.

Von Hofe, E., et al. Inhibition of N-nitrosomethylbenzylamine-induced esophageal neoplasms by the Bowman-Birk protease inhibitor. Carcinogenesis 12:2147-2150, 1991.

Watanabe, T. et al. Induction of in vitro differentiation of mouse erythroleukemia cells by genistein, an inhibitor of protein kinases. Cancer Res 51:764-768, 1991.

Watanabe, Y., et al. a case-control study of cancer of the rectum and the colon. Nippon Shokakibyo Gakkai Zasshi 81:185-193, 1984.

Welshons, WV, et al. a sensitive bioassay for detection of dietary estrogens in animal feeds. J Vet Diagn Invest 2:268-273, 1990.

Willis, KJ, et al. Recurrent breast cancer treated with the anti-estrogen tamoxifen: correlation between hormonal changes and clinical course. br Med J 1:425-428, 1977.

Witschi, H., et al. Modulation of lung tumor development in mice with the soybean-derived Bowman-Birt protease inhibitor. Carcinogenesis 10:2275-2277, 1989.

Wong E, et al. The oestrogenic activity of red clover isoflavones and some of their degradation products. J Endocrinol 24:341-348, 1962.

You W-C, et al. Diet and high risk of stomach cancer in Shandong, China. Cancer Res 48:3518-3523, 1988.

Yun T-K. Usefulness of medium-term bioassay determining formations of pulmonary edema in NIH (GP- mice for finding anti-carcinogenic agents from natural products. J Toxicol 16 (Suppl 1): 53-62, 1991.